advances in medicine

Antibiotics

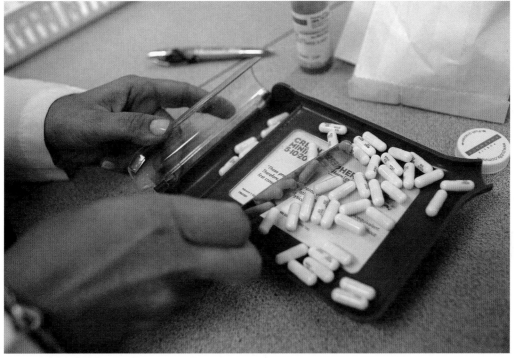

Kristi Lew

Cavendish Square
New York

Published in 2014 by Cavendish Square Publishing, LLC
303 Park Avenue South, Suite 1247, New York, NY 10010

First Edition

Website: cavendishsq.com

This publication represents the opinions and views of the author based on his or her personal experience, knowledge, and research. The information in this book serves as a general guide only. The author and publisher have used their best efforts in preparing this book and disclaim liability rising directly or indirectly from the use and application of this book.

CPSIA Compliance Information: Batch #WS13CSQ

All websites were available and accurate when this book was sent to press.

Library of Congress Cataloging-in-Publication Data
Lew, Kristi.
Antibiotics / Kristi Lew.
p. cm. – (Advances in medicine)
Includes bibliographical references and index.
Summary: "Discusses the advances that have been made in antibiotics"–Provided by publisher.
ISBN 978-1-60870-465-1 (hardcover) ISBN 978-1-62712-008-1 (paperback) ISBN 978-1-60870-593-1 (ebook)
1. Antibiotics–Juvenile literature. I. Title. II. Series.
RM267.L49 2012
615'.329–dc22
2010044009

Editors: Megan Comerford / Joyce Stanton / Christine Florie
Art Director: Anahid Hamparian   Series Designer: Nancy Sabato

Photo research by Edward Thomas
Cover: A microscopic view of penicillin mold spores and hyphae.

Cover photo by *Getty Images: David Scharf/Science Faction.*
The photographs in this book are used by permission and through the courtesy of:
Getty Images: Joe Raedle, 1; Custom Medical Stock Photo, 4; Dr. Fred Hossler/Visuals Unlimited, 23; Dr. Jack Bostrack/Visuals Unlimited, 32; Daniel Hurst Photography, 35; David Scharf, 47; Karen Kasmauski, 50; Hans Gelderblom, 55; *Alamy*: © Medical-on-Line, 7; © blickwinkel, 14; © Everett Collection Inc., 26; *Newscom*: Frank Geisler/Medicalpicture, 8; Kent Wood/Custom Medical Stock Photo, 19; Custom Medical Stock Photo, 21; J.L. Carson, 28; Dennis Kunkel, 38; 42; Custom Medical Stock Photo, 48; Portrait of Anton Van Leeuwenhoek (colour litho), Seidler, Ned M. (20th Century) / National Geographic Image Collection / The Bridgeman Art Library International, 17.

Printed in the United States of America

contents

chapter 1

A Remarkable Medical Advance

Have you ever had an ear infection? Many people have. In fact, after the common cold, ear infections are the most frequent reason kids end up in the doctor's office. Many of these infections are caused by tiny living creatures called **bacteria**.

Antibiotics are often used to treat ear infections and other illnesses.

When you have an ear infection, a doctor may prescribe medicine called an **antibiotic**. One of the more common antibiotics prescribed for ear infections is amoxicillin (referred to as the "pink stuff" by many parents). Amoxicillin and other antibiotics are medicines that can kill or slow the growth of bacteria.

Today, the use of antibiotics is fairly common. However, this has not always been the case. Before penicillin became widely available in the early 1940s, many people died from bacterial infections.

What Are Bacteria?

Bacteria are tiny living organisms made up of only one cell. They are so small that they cannot be seen without the help of a microscope. Bacteria and other organisms too small to be seen with the naked eye are called **microorganisms**, or microbes. Sometimes people call them germs. Viruses, fungi, and protozoans are types of microbes, too. When any of these germs invade the body, they may cause an infection and make the person sick.

Biologists do not classify bacteria as animals or plants. Instead, bacteria belong in a group all their own. When only one cell is present, it is called a bacterium. But bacteria are rarely found alone. They group together, sometimes by the millions. And they multiply very, very quickly.

There are thousands of types of bacteria in the world. Most of them are harmless or even helpful to humans, but not all of them. Some types of bacteria can make people very sick. Tuberculosis and pneumonia–infections of the lungs–are caused by bacteria. So are strep throat, Lyme disease, and most types of food poisoning. Bacteria that can make people sick are called **pathogenic** bacteria.

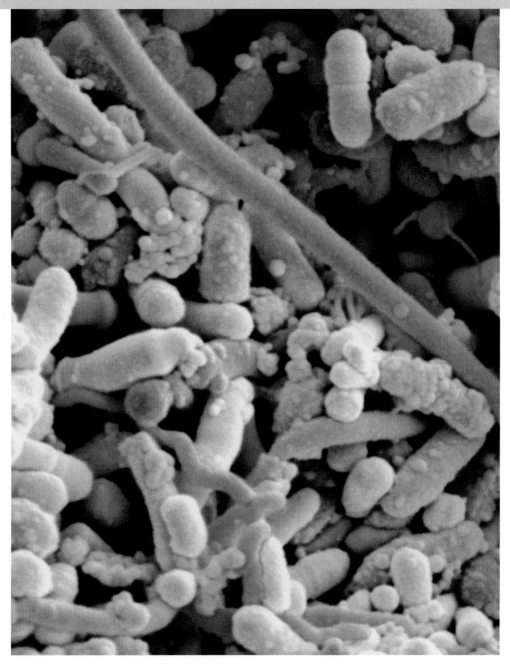

Bacteria are tiny, single-celled organisms. They come in many different shapes, but a powerful microscope is needed to make them large enough to see.

Leukocytes (blue) travel through the bloodstream tagging invading microorganisms for destruction.

The Immune System

When bacteria enter the human body, they trigger the body's **immune system**. Special white blood cells, called **leukocytes**, are a part of the immune system. Leukocytes travel around the body in the bloodstream searching for and destroying invading bacteria and other microorganisms. There are two main types of leukocytes: phagocytes and lymphocytes.

There are two types of lymphocytes in the human body: B cells and T cells. B cells and T cells have different jobs to do. Bacteria and other microbes have chemicals on their surfaces called **antigens**. When a B cell encounters an antigen, it remembers that particular surface chemical. The next time the B cell finds an invading cell with that antigen, it immediately recognizes it as an intruder and makes antibodies. The **antibodies** that the B cell makes are specific to the antigen on the surface of the bacteria. The antibodies themselves do not destroy the invading microbe. Instead, they lock on to the specific antigen like a key. By doing this, they target the cell for destruction by other immune cells.

This is where the T cells and phagocytes come into the picture. Some T cells, called killer cells, destroy cells tagged with antibodies. Other types of T cells help alert phagocytes that their assistance is needed. Phagocytes surround and destroy foreign particles tagged by the B and T cells. There are several different types of phagocytes circulating throughout a healthy human body. Different types of phagocytes combat different types of intruders. The most common type of phagocyte is called a neutrophil.

As you can see, your body is well equipped to defend itself against invading germs. However, there are times when the immune system just cannot

IMMUNIZATION

Before you entered school, most likely you were required to get a series of shots to prevent certain diseases. Each shot introduced your immune system to a particular antigen in a way that would not make you sick. Alerting your B cells to these antigens would allow them to make antibodies quickly if the antigens were to be encountered again. You would now be immunized against the disease.

WHY ARE THEY CALLED B AND T CELLS?

Lymphocytes are made and stored in different parts of the body. B cells are made in the bone marrow. The other type of lymphocytes also start out in the bone marrow, but they soon move to the thymus, where they mature into T cells. The thymus is a gland located just behind the top of the breastbone. Its function is to make mature T cells that are ready to battle intruders in order to keep the body healthy. The *b* in *bone marrow* and the *t* in *thymus* are where these very important immune cells get their names.

keep up. When this happens, your doctor might prescribe medicine to help the immune system protect the body. If the illness is caused by bacteria, the doctor is most likely to prescribe an antibiotic.

What Are Antibiotics?

The word *antibiotic* comes from two Greek words: *anti*, which means "against," and *bios*, which means "life." An antibiotic, therefore, is something that prevents, slows down, or destroys life. Antibiotics are naturally occurring substances made from fungi or other types of microorganisms that kill bacteria or stop them from growing. Scientists have discovered techniques that allow them to duplicate some of these naturally occurring substances in the laboratory. Technically, these synthetic medications are called **antibacterials**. However, most people (including many scientists and doctors) commonly call these laboratory-produced chemicals antibiotics.

Antibiotics and antibacterials belong to a larger classification of drugs called **antimicrobials**. Scientists have also discovered drugs to fight other types of microbes besides bacteria. **Antiviral** medications stop viruses from reproducing. Antifungal or antiparasitic drugs are used when the body needs help to eliminate a fungal or parasitic infection.

There are two major classes of antibiotics: broad-spectrum and narrow-spectrum. Broad-spectrum antibiotics treat a wide variety of bacterial infections. Narrow-spectrum antibiotics fight only a few specific types of bacteria.

Different antibiotics are used for different types of bacterial infections. Before prescribing an antibiotic, doctors usually conduct laboratory tests to determine what type of bacteria is making a person sick. This is the reason you should never take an antibiotic prescribed for someone else. Even if that person has the same symptoms as you, it is possible that a different kind of bacteria is the cause. At best, the antibiotic will not help, and at worst, it could be harmful.

Antibiotics are a remarkable medical advance. When taken as directed by a doctor, they can do more than make someone feel better: they can save a person's life.

chapter 2

How Antibiotics Were Discovered

More than three thousand years ago, the ancient Chinese smeared moldy tofu on skin infections. They did not do this because they knew about antibiotics. They didn't know that bacteria were the cause of the skin infections, either. They didn't even know that bacteria existed! But they did know that anyone suffering from a particular type of skin infection got better when moldy tofu was spread on the wound.

A chemical in the bark of the cinochona tree prevents reproduction in the microorganism that causes malaria.

The ancient Chinese were not the only ones to experiment with natural substances to ward off infection. To keep wounds from becoming infected, for example, the ancient Greeks tried covering them with a mixture of ground onion, myrrh oil, honey, and wine. The ancient Egyptians, with some success, tried pressing moldy bread against the gashes of their wounded.

The native peoples of South America also used natural antimicrobial agents. They discovered that chewing the bark of a cinchona tree could help reduce the fever caused by a bout of malaria. They also discovered that wearing mold-covered sandals could relieve a foot infection. Like the ancient Chinese, Greeks, and Egyptians, however, the South Americans did not understand why these treatments worked as they did.

Germ Theory of Disease

The tiny creatures causing the infections treated by the furry sandals and moldy bread and tofu were not discovered for thousands of years. Antoni van Leeuwenhoek, the man who is credited with the discovery of bacteria in the 1600s, did not start out to be a scientist. In fact, he worked in a dry-goods store. While working in the store, Leeuwenhoek would sometimes use a magnifying glass to count the threads in clothing.

Although he had no formal training in science, Leeuwenhoek did possess a powerful sense of curiosity and strong observational skills. At some point, he became interested in grinding and polishing his own magnifying lenses, and he soon excelled at the art. In fact, some of his lenses could magnify objects 270 times their original size. With this magnification, he was able to see all kinds of tiny, never-seen-before objects, including bacteria, which he described in 1676.

Antoni van Leeuwenhoek was the first scientist to observe and describe bacteria.

However, Leeuwenhoek had no idea that the tiny creatures he was observing with his simple microscope were capable of causing human disease. The link between bacteria and human illness would not be made for more than 160 years. In 1840 a German physician, Friedrich Gustav Jakob Henle, published the first scientific paper suggesting that infectious diseases might be caused by living microorganisms.

Ten years later, veterinarian Pierre Rayer and physician Franz Antoine Pollender independently observed that animals dying of anthrax—a disease common in cattle and sheep—all had large, rod-shaped bacteria in their blood. However, it was not until 1876 that Robert Koch, a German physician and student of Henle, was able to prove that the bacteria *Bacillus anthracis* caused anthrax. Koch developed a very specific list of rules that could be used to determine if a particular microorganism caused a specific disease. These steps became known as Koch's postulates.

Koch's postulates, along with the work of other scientists including Louis Pasteur and Joseph Lister, helped cement the idea that germs cause disease. Koch went on to discover the bacteria that cause tuberculosis, and his research laid the groundwork for other scientists' discoveries. Between 1879 and 1889 scientists discovered the different types of bacteria that cause diseases such as cholera, typhoid fever, diphtheria, pneumonia, tetanus, and meningitis.

Discovery of Penicillin

One of Koch's postulates requires that scientists be able to grow bacteria in the laboratory. Koch and other scientists maintained that the only way to truly study and understand the nature of a particular microbe was to grow

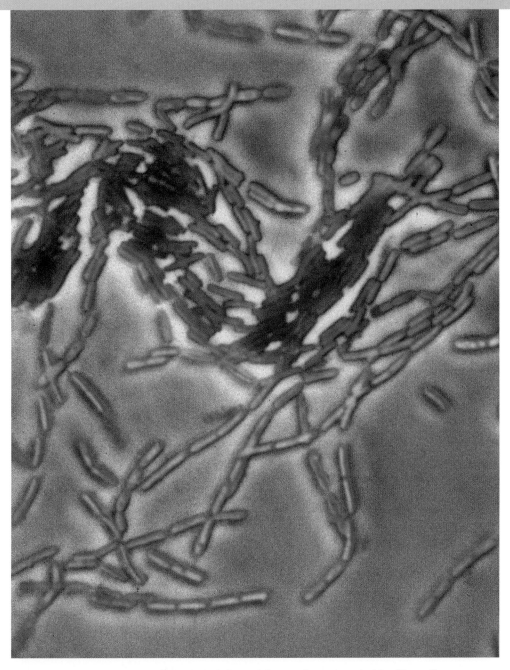

The bacteria that causes anthrax is rod-shaped. It was first observed by Pierre Rayer and Franz Antoine Pollender in 1850.

KOCH'S POSTULATES

Koch's postulates are a set of four rules used to determine if a particular microorganism causes a specific disease:

1. The microorganism must be present in all cases of the disease.

2. The microorganism must be isolated from the organism with the disease and grown in the laboratory.

3. When a healthy and susceptible laboratory animal is exposed to the microorganism grown in the laboratory, it must develop the same symptoms of the disease.

4. The microorganism isolated from the test animal must be identical to the microorganism isolated from the original diseased animal.

a pure culture of it. A pure culture is one that contains only a single type of microorganism. To grow a pure culture of a particular bacterium, a scientist places a sample of it in a small, shallow, loosely covered dish, called a petri dish. He or she also places a gelatinlike substance called agar in the petri dish. Agar contains all of the nutrients the bacteria need to grow.

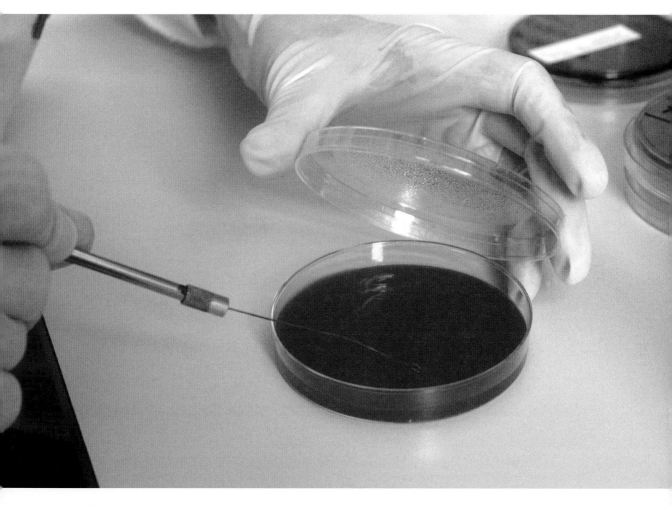

To grow bacteria in the laboratory, a scientist must provide it with the nutrients it needs.

In 1928 Alexander Fleming, a Scottish biologist, was growing pure cultures of the bacteria *Staphylococcus aureus*, which causes staph infections. He needed the pure cultures to advance his research on effective antiseptics. An antiseptic is a substance that can destroy disease-causing organisms without harming healthy body tissue.

One day, before throwing away some bacterial cultures that had become contaminated with mold, Fleming noticed that some of the cultures had a strange appearance. Around the mold were bacteria-free zones. The mold had killed the bacteria.

Fleming took a sample of the mold and determined that it belonged to the genus *Penicillium*. He named the active ingredient in the mold—the substance that killed the bacteria—penicillin. Fleming published his findings in 1929, but not many people took an interest in his research. He went on to study the mold for many years, but he was never able to develop an easy technique for growing and purifying it.

Sulfa Drugs

The same year that Fleming published his work about penicillin, three other scientists—Gerhard Domagk, Fritz Mietzsch, and Joseph Klarer—were working on ways in which chemical red dyes might be used medicinally. In 1931 they tested a chemically altered red dye called prontosil rubrum in rabbits and mice with infections caused by *Streptococcus* bacteria. The prontosil killed the bacteria, and the animals got better.

It is unclear exactly when prontosil was used for the first time in humans. Some stories say that the new drug was administered to a ten-month-old boy suffering from a deadly blood infection in 1933. Other stories claim

Alexander Fleming found that *Penicillium notatum*, a mold, has a powerful antibiotic effect.

that, the year before, it was Domagk's own daughter who developed a potentially deadly infection after pricking her hand with a needle. After her father gave her a dose of the new drug, she recovered completely. Prontosil became widely known in the United States in 1936 when it was given to President Franklin D. Roosevelt's son Franklin Jr., who was suffering from a streptococcal infection.

Even though the drug was working in animals and humans, scientists continued to get some strange results that they did not understand. Prontosil only worked when it was injected. It would not kill bacteria in a test tube. Only later did a team of French scientists discover that when the drug is injected into a mammal, the animal's liver changes the chemical makeup of the prontosil. In the liver, prontosil is broken down into an active sulfur-containing antibiotic called sulfanilamide. The scientists quickly realized that sulfanilamide had been discovered, described, and patented long before. In 1908 Austrian chemist Paul Gelmo had reported his discovery of sulfanilamide, a chemical stepping-stone in the dye-making process. However, Gelmo did not realize the medicinal uses of the chemical. By the time the French research team discovered that sulfanilamide was the active breakdown product of prontosil, Gelmo's patent on the chemical had expired and anyone could make and sell it. This was good for patients who needed the drug, because sulfanilamide was significantly less expensive to produce than prontosil.

Widespread Antibiotic Use

The success of sulfanilamide made pharmaceutical companies and doctors eager to find other sulfa drugs that could treat bacterial infections.

Throughout the late 1930s and early 1940s, scientists developed a number of such medications. One of these drugs, sulfapyridine, was used to treat British prime minister Winston Churchill when he developed pneumonia during World War II. Sulfathiazole was another newly discovered drug that could treat pneumonia and streptococcal infections. The use of these and other sulfa drugs spread rapidly.

The late 1930s saw not only the emergence of sulfa drugs. It was also the time when Fleming's penicillin reappeared. In 1938, nine years after Fleming's publication of his results, three scientists—Howard Florey, Ernst Chain, and Norman Heatley—finally succeeded in growing, extracting, and purifying penicillin from mold cultures. Five years later, with the help of pharmaceutical companies, the scientists were able to develop a method of producing enough of the antibiotic to make a financially viable drug.

It was not until 1942 that the term *antibiotic* came into use. The word was introduced by an American scientist named Selman Waksman. Waksman went on to discover the antibiotic streptomycin in 1944. This powerful antibiotic was the first to be used to combat tuberculosis. Later, scientists found that the drug was also effective against other illnesses, such as bubonic plague, cholera, typhoid fever, and urinary tract infections. In 1952 Waksman was awarded the Nobel Prize in Medicine for his discovery.

In the 1950s and 1960s, antibiotic research continued, and many different classes of new antibiotics were discovered. Vancomycin, a powerful antibiotic still in use today, for example, was derived from soil bacteria found in the rain forests of Borneo in 1956. And in 1960 scientists introduced a semisynthetic derivative of penicillin called methicillin. Other common antibiotics related to penicillin include ampicillin, amoxicillin, and benzylpenicillin.

Selmen Waksman discovered the antibiotic streptomycin in 1944. This powerful antibiotic has been effective in treating tuberculosis, bubonic plague, cholera, and other bacterial infections.

By the 1980s and 1990s, scientists were able to improve on many of the classes of antibiotics that had already been discovered, but the rate of discovery had slowed significantly by the late twentieth and early twenty-first centuries.

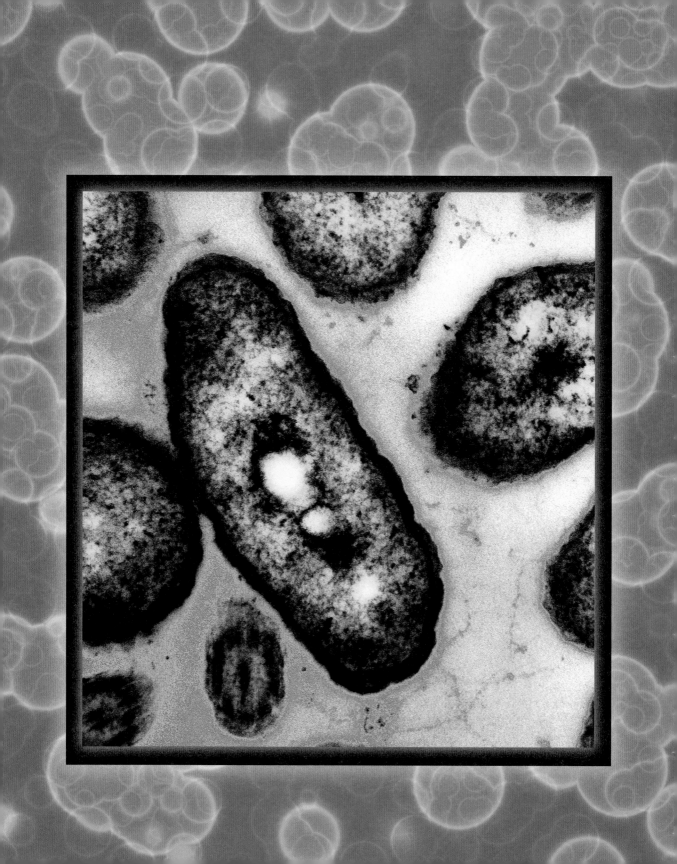

chapter 3

How Antibiotics Work

**M**any of the illnesses and wounds that doctors treat with antibiotics today could have easily killed someone only seventy years ago. Even if a person's immune system was strong and the individual did not die from a bacterial infection back then, he or she was often left with permanent disabilities. Antibacterial drugs were introduced in the United States in 1936. The result was revolutionary. The widespread use of antibiotics has saved thousands of lives, made surgery and childbirth much safer, and helped curb devastating diseases. How do these amazing drugs work?

Whooping cough is a highly contagious bacterial infection that causes severe, uncontrollable coughing. It was a common and deadly disease in infants until a vaccine to prevent it was introduced in the 1930s.

Selective Poisons

Antibiotics are selective poisons. They target bacterial cells without harming the sick person's body cells. Like the natural antibodies made by the body, an antibiotic searches out a particular pattern of chemicals on the bacteria's surface. Also like natural antibodies, not every antibiotic will combat every kind of bacteria. If the antibiotic "key" does not fit into the bacteria's surface chemical's "lock," the antibiotic will not work.

Different antibiotics work on their target bacteria in different ways. Sometimes an antibiotic kills the bacteria outright. These antibiotics are called **bactericides**. Other types of antibiotics do not kill the bacteria; instead, they interfere with the way the bacteria reproduce. Keeping the bacteria from multiplying out of control gives the body's immune system time to kill the bacteria. These are called **bacteriostatic** antibiotics.

One way a bacteriostatic antibiotic might keep bacteria from reproducing is to interfere with the way bacteria construct their cell walls. When bacteria reproduce, they split into two cells, called daughter cells. Each daughter cell must have its own cell wall. Some antibiotics, including penicillin, disrupt the bacteria's cell wall-making machinery. Without the ability to make new cell walls, daughter cells cannot form, and the bacteria cannot reproduce.

Not all bacteria have cell walls. The antibiotic erythromycin can be effective against these kinds of pathogens. Erythromycin is often used for illnesses such as bacterial bronchitis and whooping cough. Erythromycin and similar antibiotics work by disrupting the way bacteria make proteins. In small doses these antibiotics can stop bacteria from multiplying; in larger doses they can kill bacteria outright.

Prontosil and other sulfa drugs also interfere with the ability of bacteria to reproduce. In order to reproduce, bacteria must copy their genetic material so they can pass it on to their daughter cells. The sulfanilamides disrupt this copying process.

Nitrofurantoin, an antibiotic sometimes used to treat urinary tract infections, targets bacteria in yet another way. It prevents bacteria from converting glucose (sugar) into energy. Without energy, the cell dies.

Sometimes a doctor might prescribe two different types of antibiotics in combination. For example, by combining a bactericide with a bacteriostatic antibiotic, doctors can more effectively treat certain bacterial infections, allowing patients to feel better faster.

Gram Staining

Most of the antibacterials produced today attack gram-positive bacteria. Both gram-positive and gram-negative bacteria have cell walls. However, their cell walls are constructed differently. Almost all bacteria can be classified as either gram-positive or gram-negative, depending on the results of a staining method called the Gram stain test. This method of identifying types of bacteria was developed in 1884 by Hans Christian Gram, a Danish physician. Gram developed the test after he noticed that the lungs of patients who had died of bacterial pneumonia were more likely to take up particular stains.

Gram staining allows bacteria, which are usually transparent, to be viewed easily under a microscope. To stain bacteria, a slide with a bacterial smear is first flooded with a chemical called crystal violet. The cell membranes of gram-positive bacteria will absorb and retain this dark purple stain. However, gram-negative bacteria have a secondary outer

Gram-positive bacteria turn dark purple with Gram stain. Gram-negative bacteria will not absorb the stain. They appear pink.

membrane that will not retain the purple dye. To complete the Gram stain test, a counterstain is applied to make gram-negative bacteria easier to see. The counterstain is absorbed by the gram-negative bacteria's outer membranes and makes them appear pink under a microscope.

The secondary membrane present in gram-negative bacteria not only makes it harder for crystal violet to penetrate their cell walls; it also makes it harder for antibiotics to affect gram-negative bacteria. Therefore, doctors have fewer drugs from which to choose when treating a gram-negative bacterial infection.

Antiviral Drugs

Antibiotics only work on infections caused by bacteria. They have no effect on infections that are caused by viruses. The common cold, flu, rabies, and mononucleosis are infections caused by viruses. Doctors do not prescribe antibiotics for someone suffering from a cold because the drugs would do no good. However, doctors have other drugs, called antiviral drugs, which sometimes can be used to combat a virus. Like antibiotics, however, antiviral drugs only work on the viruses they were designed for.

Unlike bacteria, viruses are not considered to be living organisms. In order for a virus to reproduce, it must invade the cell of another living creature. The living creature that the virus invades is called a host. Viruses cannot reproduce on their own because they do not have the chemicals necessary to copy their genetic material. Once they infect the cells of the host, they take over and use the copying chemicals in those cells, forcing the host cells to make more viruses.

HELPFUL BACTERIA

Not all bacteria make people sick. In fact, these tiny organisms can be quite helpful. Scientists have figured out how to use bacteria to make, or help make, some medicines, **hormones**, and antibodies that can keep people healthy. Bacteria that naturally live in the human intestine help us digest our food. Bacteria that live in oxygen-free environments, such as swamps, landfills, and areas deep in the earth, produce methane gas, which is the main component of natural gas. (People use natural gas to heat their homes.) Bacteria are needed to make yogurt, sour cream, and most cheeses. Pharmaceutical companies use bacteria to produce human insulin on a commercial scale.

Before scientists discovered how to insert human **DNA** (genetic material) into bacteria to produce human insulin, insulin from cows or pigs was used to treat diabetes. However, cow and pig insulin are slightly different from human insulin, and sometimes caused allergic reactions in people. Insulin is not the only drug scientists can get bacteria to make. Some types of bacteria can be used to make antibiotics that doctors can prescribe to fight infections caused by other types of bacteria. Therefore, when we hear the word *bacteria*, we should not immediately assume the microorganisms are harmful.

Some antiviral medications work by preventing the virus from hijacking the host cell's chemical-copying mechanisms. Without the chemicals, a virus cannot replicate, or make a copy of itself. Most of the drugs used to treat people infected with the human immunodeficiency virus (HIV) work this way.

Other types of antiviral drugs work by strengthening the body's own immune system response. Many vaccines work this way. A vaccine contains a dead or weakened virus. When a person is vaccinated, the virus is introduced to the body's immune cells, which remember them. Then, when those immune cells see the same type of chemical combination on the surface of a new invading virus, they recognize it and quickly go on the attack. The person's immune system is able to defend itself much faster than it could have if it had never seen that virus before.

Because viruses use the host's own cells to replicate, however, it is difficult for scientists to make drugs that will target only the virus and not harm the host cells. Viruses, like bacteria, can also become resistant to the drugs used to treat them.

Bacteria Out of Control

When a bacterium reproduces, it copies its DNA. It then splits into two cells. Those two cells also reproduce to produce four cells. Four cells turn into eight cells, eight cells into sixteen cells, and so on. Scientists have found that, amazingly, a single bacterium like *Staphylococcus aureus* can produce 5 billion trillion new cells every day. In the process of the DNA being copied, mistakes are occasionally made. Mistakes, or **mutations**, in DNA can sometimes be harmful to the bacteria and cause the bacteria to die.

However, mutations can also be beneficial to the bacteria. Occasionally, mutations allow the bacteria to become antibiotic resistant; that is, they no longer respond to the drugs created to control them.

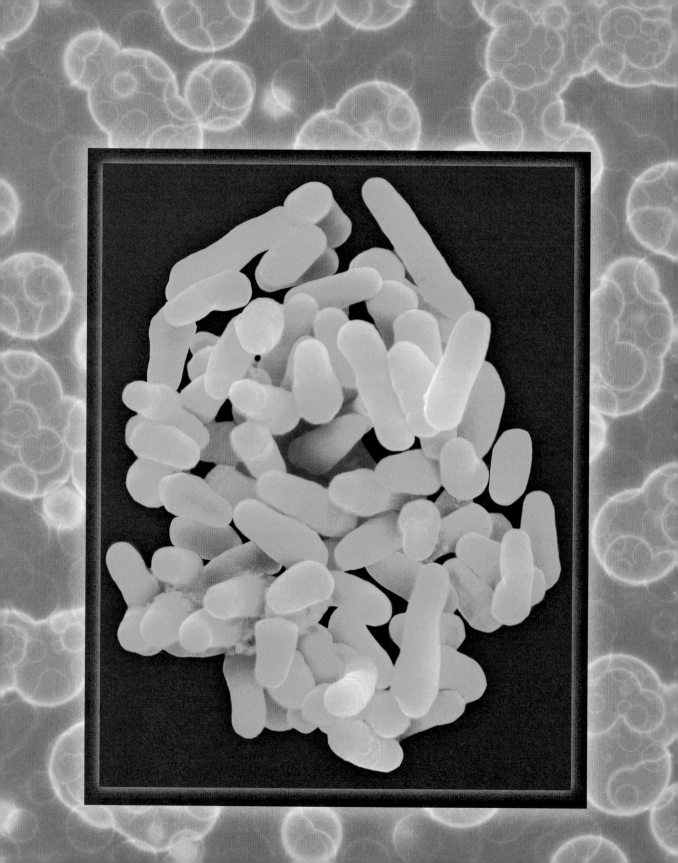

chapter 4

Antibiotic Resistance

Antibiotics, one of the greatest medical advances in history, are in danger of becoming unusable. In July 2009 the principal deputy commissioner of the U.S. Food and Drug Administration (FDA), Joshua Sharfstein, reported to Congress that every year approximately 2 million Americans acquire bacterial infections in hospitals around the country. Of those 2 million infections, Sharfstein said, some 70 percent are caused by bacteria that are resistant to at least one antibiotic. Nearly 90,000 hospital patients, he reported, die each year as a result of these bacterial infections.

Several of the antibiotics used in the past to control bacteria that cause tuberculosis no longer kill the bacteria. Antibiotic resistance is a worldwide health problem with no end in sight.

Bacteria that are resistant to more than one antibiotic are called multi-drug-resistant (MDR) bacteria. MDR bacteria are a growing problem in the health-care industry today. Even more alarming than multidrug-resistant bacteria are those that scientists have found to be resistant to *all* of the antibacterial drugs in existence.

It doesn't take long for bacteria to develop a resistance to antibiotics. Only one year after Albert Alexander, an English police officer, became the first person to be treated with penicillin, scientists identified a type of *Staphylococcus aureus* that was immune to the new "miracle drug." Today, scientists estimate that about 90 percent of *S. aureus* bacteria are resistant to penicillin.

When bacteria become resistant to the medications doctors prefer to use, which are sometimes called the "first line of defense," other antibacterials must be prescribed. It often takes longer for these second-choice drugs to control the infection. These drugs can also be more expensive and cause more side effects.

When bacteria evolve a resistance to the second-choice medications, they are called extensively drug resistant (XDR). In some areas of the world, the bacteria that cause tuberculosis (TB) have become extensively drug resistant. Cases of XDR-TB are very hard to treat. Treatment of standard, drug-sensitive (meaning the bacteria respond to the drugs) TB requires taking four different antibiotics over the course of six months. The cost of treatment is about $20, which can be high for many people in the third world. MDR-TB and XDR-TB can emerge if people infected with the bacteria do not take their medication as directed. Drug-resistant forms of TB must be treated with medications that can cause dangerous side effects. In addition, treatment can take up to two years and cost nearly $5,000.

MRSA Infections

Methicillin, the semisynthetic penicillin that was introduced in 1960, was often used to treat *S. aureus* just as penicillin was. However, a year after its introduction, doctors reported methicillin-resistant *S. aureus*, or MRSA. A study conducted in 2005 estimated that approximately 18,000 Americans die of MRSA infections every year. That same year, the number of MRSA deaths surpassed the number of people who died of AIDS.

In 1999 scientists started using a combination of other antibiotics, specifically quinupristin and dalfopristin, in an attempt to control MRSA. This one-two medical punch worked for about a year. However, in 2000 scientists found certain strains of *S. aureus* that were also resistant to the quinupristin/dalfopristin combination.

Bacteria that have developed a resistance to all known antibiotics are called **superbugs**. While superbugs are rare, many scientists believe that it is only a matter of time before more superbugs emerge. In August 2010 a bacterium with a gene called New Delhi metallo-beta-lactamase 1, or NDM-1, was discovered in the United Kingdom. So far any bacteria with this gene seem to be resistant to nearly all of the antibiotics tested. Scientists are keeping a close eye on this gene and on the bacteria that have it.

Another potential superbug is called vancomycin-intermediate/resistant *Staphylococcus aureus*, or VISA. VISA is resistant to many antibiotics, including vancomycin, one of the most powerful antibiotics that doctors have to combat bacterial infections. This strain of bacteria has shown up in hospitals around the world.

Hospitals are not the only places where drug-resistant bacteria thrive.

SUPERBUG GENE

Discovered in pneumonia and E.coli bugs resistant to last-line antibiotics

NDM-1

- Produces an enzyme that counteracts effect of antibiotics

- Found in India, Pakistan, Bangladesh and Britain

- Many of the patients had visited India or Pakistan for cosmetic surgery

- Alarm over gene's apparent ability to replicate across bacterial species

The NDM-1 gene contains the instructions to make a chemical that prevents the antibiotic that targets it from working. Scientists are concerned because they believe the NDM-1 gene can be passed from one bacterium to another.

In fact, MRSA has been reported in schools across the nation, too. When an infection occurs in a hospital, doctors term the condition "care associated." These infections are usually related to invasive procedures such as surgery, joint replacement, or intravenous tubing. The type of infection that occurs outside the hospital is called a **community-acquired**, or community-associated, infection. Community-acquired MRSA (CA-MRSA) infections are spread by skin-to-skin contact and are often associated with school athletes, child-care workers, and people who live in crowded housing. CA-MRSA often appears initially as a painful, pus-filled, blisterlike area on the skin.

How Do Bacteria Become Resistant?

Some bacteria may have a natural resistance to a particular antibiotic. In other words, unlike other bacteria of the same type, particular bacteria may possess a slightly different genetic code that makes them resistant to a specific antibiotic. This genetic code may change the pattern of chemicals on the bacteria's surface. When that happens, the antibiotic can no longer find and destroy the bacteria.

Another way bacteria may become resistant to antibiotics is through genetic mutations. Like natural resistance, a mutation may change the bacteria so that an antibiotic no longer recognizes it. A mutation also may give the bacteria the ability to chemically alter the antibiotic itself, rendering the drug useless. Mutations that give bacteria antibiotic resistance are rare. However, when one bacterium can produce 5 billion trillion new cells every day, there are a lot of chances for genetic mutations to take place.

Spontaneous mutations such as these are not the only way DNA can change in bacteria. Scientists have found that resistant bacteria can

ANTIBIOTIC RESISTANCE TIMELINE

1941 Penicillin given to first patient.

1942 Penicillin-resistant bacteria reported.

1956 Vancomycin used for the first time.

1960 Methicillin approved for use in patients.

1961 Methicillin-resistant bacteria reported.

1992 Vancomycin-resistant gene moves from *Enterococci* bacteria to *Staphylococcus aureus.*

1997 Vancomycin-intermediate/resistant *Staphylococcus aureus,* or VISA, reported.

1999 Doctors start using a combination of quinupristin and dalfopristin to control MRSA.

2000 *Staphylococcus aureus* shows resistance to quinupristin/dalfopristin drug combination.

2002 Full vancomycin-resistant bacteria reported.

2005 Tigecycline introduced and, so far, seems to be working to combat MRSA infections.

2007 Resistance to tigecycline by *Acinetobacter baumannii* reported. This type of bacteria, nicknamed "Iraqibacter" because it has caused so many infections in American soldiers wounded in Iraq, is resistant to most other antibiotics as well.

2010 Bacteria with the gene New Delhi metallo-beta-lactamase 1, or NDM-1, discovered in the United Kingdom. Bacteria with this gene seem to be resistant to nearly all of the antibiotics tested.

sometimes transfer the genes that make them resistant to other bacteria. This type of gene transfer, known as horizontal gene transfer, can occur in three ways: conjugation, transformation, or transduction.

Conjunction occurs when two bacteria come into contact with each other and small pieces of DNA, called **plasmids**, are transferred. The gene NDM-1, found in the new superbug discovered in August 2010, for example, has been found on plasmids. Transformation occurs when a bacterium takes up DNA that it finds in the environment. The DNA is usually free in the environment due to the death of other bacteria. And transduction occurs when a virus that infects bacteria transfers drug-resistant DNA from one bacterium to another.

Multidrug-Resistant Bacteria

Antibiotic-resistant bacterial strains come about when bacteria are exposed repeatedly to an antibiotic. At first the antibiotic is successful in killing its intended target, but occasionally a bacterium will carry genetic material that prevents the antibiotic from working. When that bacterium reproduces, it makes more bacteria that carry the resistant genes. The resulting bacteria are resistant to that particular antibiotic. If a patient is then given a different antibiotic, it is possible that one of the surviving bacterium also carries a gene that makes it resistant to this second drug. If it survives and reproduces, it becomes multidrug-resistant (MDR) bacteria.

Many scientists and doctors believe that the increase in the number of MDR bacterial infections in hospitals and in the community has been compounded by the overprescription of antibiotics. They believe that this

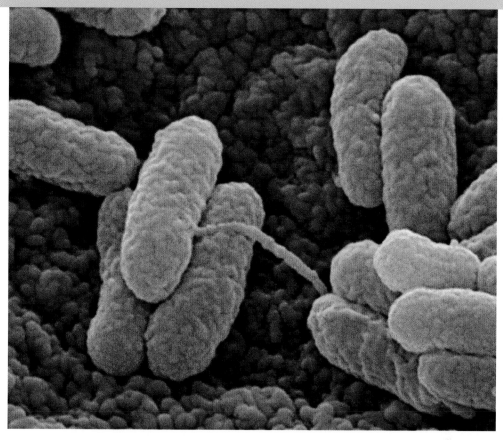

One bacterial cell can transfer genetic material to another through a bridge-like connection called a conjugation pilus.

practice has given bacteria more contact with the drugs and caused the bacteria to rapidly evolve drug resistances.

Doctors are often faced with patients demanding an antibiotic for an illness, even when taking an antibiotic is not the best option for that illness or that patient. For example, going to the doctor and expecting him or her to prescribe an antibiotic for a cold is not realistic. Colds are caused by viruses. Taking an antibiotic for a cold will not get rid of the cold. In fact,

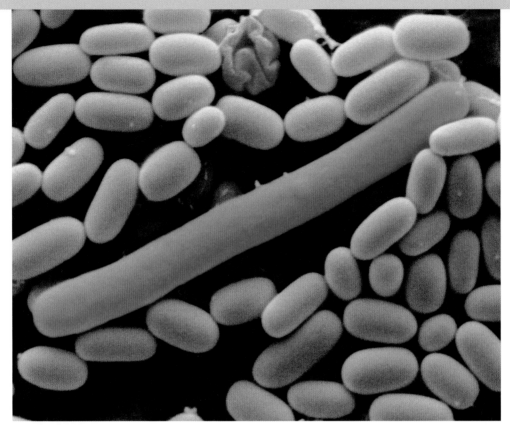

Clostridium difficile (green) is a bacteria that can grow out of control when the normal intestinal bacteria are destroyed.

it could lead to more problems for that patient as well as for public health, because it exposes bacteria that normally live in the body to the antibiotic. If these bacteria develop antibiotic resistance, they could pass the DNA code for the resistance on to other, more dangerous types of bacteria.

There are other reasons not to take antibiotics unless they are really needed. Antibiotics are considered safe drugs, but this is not always the case. People can have allergic reactions to them. Sometimes these allergic reactions can be severe, and severe allergic reactions can be life threatening.

Antibiotics can have side effects. The most common side effects are upset stomach and diarrhea. Antibiotics can also interact with other drugs. Taking antibiotics in combination with birth control pills, for example, can make the birth control pills ineffective.

Antibiotics can also upset the natural balance of bacteria in the body, leading to yeast infections, digestive imbalances, and other problems. For example, *Clostridium difficile* infections in the United States are on the rise. *C. difficile*, often called *C. diff*, is a bacterium that can thrive in the human intestinal tract. Under normal circumstances, *C. diff* bacteria that enter the intestinal tract are kept in check by the bacteria that live there naturally. However, if a course of broad-spectrum antibiotics has killed the natural, "good" intestinal bacteria, *C. diff* can flourish, causing severe diarrhea and making the person very ill. In addition, many strains of *C. diff* have become resistant to the antibiotics used to control them.

chapter 5

The Future
of Antibiotics

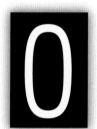 verprescription of antibiotics in humans is not the only factor contributing to the creation of antibiotic-resistant bacteria. Overprescription of antibiotics in animals—particularly animals that enter the food chain—has scientists increasingly troubled.

Using antibiotics to treat sick animals is necessary. However, giving antibiotics to healthy food animals can endanger human health. Farmers in Norway have successfully eliminated most antibiotics in dairy cows by changing their living conditions.

Antibiotic Use in Animals

Sometimes antibiotics are necessary to treat a bacterial infection in a sick animal. They are also used to protect healthy animals in close contact with sick ones. However, this is not the only way antibiotics are used on farms today. Antibiotics are also used to ward off the possibility of infection (even if no infection is present) and to promote growth. Using antibiotics to promote growth in animals is good economically for a farmer who can produce larger animals in less time. It is not good in terms of human health.

The World Health Organization (WHO) estimates that nearly half of the antibiotics produced worldwide are consumed by food animals. This is just an estimate, however, because records of exactly how many and which types of antibiotics are used on humans and on animals are not available for all countries. But the link between antibiotic use in food animals and the emergence of antibiotic-resistant bacteria has been well documented. For example, after a new class of antibiotics called fluoroquinolones was introduced in poultry production, several studies in the United States and the United Kingdom found an increase in fluoroquinolone-resistant bacteria in the animals. Not long after that, fluoroquinolone-resistant *Salmonella* and *Campylobacter*—bacteria that cause food poisoning in humans—were also found in the human population. Use of fluoroquinolones in poultry production in the United States was banned in 2005.

To combat the overprescription of antibiotics in animals, many nations have already taken action. In 1997, for example, the European Union (EU) banned all antibiotics used in human medicine from being used as growth promoters in animals. Sweden has even stricter nontherapeutic antimicrobial legislation. In 1986 the country banned all use of growth promoters in animals, whether the drugs are used in human medicine or not. In 1999 Denmark banned all nontherapeutic use of antibiotics in animals. In 2000 Switzerland passed similar laws. In 2011, South Korea became the first country in Asia to ban antibiotics in animal feed. As of the writing of this book, however, the United States has no such law.

In June 2010 the FDA released new recommendations that suggest limiting the use of certain antibiotics in animals. According to Donald Kennedy, a former commissioner of the FDA, this is not the first attempt by the agency to limit such use. Kennedy reported to the *New York Times* that the agency has known for more than thirty years that the nontherapeutic use of antibiotics in food animals was tied to the emergence of antibiotic-resistant bacteria. The FDA has tried repeatedly to limit the use of antibiotics as growth promoters in animal feed, including the introduction of a voluntary program in 2012. However, Congress—after prompting from the agricultural industry—has prevented any regulations that would address this issue.

While banning the use of antibiotics as growth promoters is a step in the right direction, it will not eliminate the emergence of antibiotic-resistant bacteria on the farm. Depending on who is asked, the percentage of known antibiotics used on farms can vary widely. The Union of Concerned Scientists, for example, told a *New York Times* reporter that in 2001 farmers used about 84 percent of all the known antibiotics. They estimated that approximately 70 percent of those were used to promote animal growth or to prevent the spread of bacteria to healthy animals raised in crowded feedlots. However, the Animal Health Institute, an agricultural trade group, told the same *New York Times* reporter that only about 13 percent of the antibiotics used by farmers are targeted to promoting growth.

Beyond Antibiotics

Pharmaceutical companies are working on the development of new antibiotics, but this process takes time and money. Many scientists believe that if we are to succeed at defeating pathogenic bacteria, new classes of antibiotics will need to be created. In other words, we need an antibiotic that will work in a different way from the ones currently on the market.

Another way to potentially combat pathogenic bacteria is to make use of the natural interaction between viruses and bacteria. Viruses that infect bacteria are called **bacteriophages**. The viruses target and kill bacterial cells without harming people or animals. Called phage therapy, this technique has already been successfully used on patients in some parts of the world. In fact, scientists in the former Soviet republic of Georgia have been researching this therapy since the 1920s.

Before the widespread use of antibiotics, phage therapy was also used in the United States. Now, with the emergence of more and more multidrug-resistant bacterial strains, scientists are once again looking into this potential treatment. One advantage that bacteriophages have over antibiotics is that, like bacteria, viruses can evolve very quickly. Therefore, a bacterium that has evolved to be resistant to a particular phage may find itself facing a phage that has also evolved a different way to kill it.

The key disadvantage to using bacteriophages to treat bacterial infec-

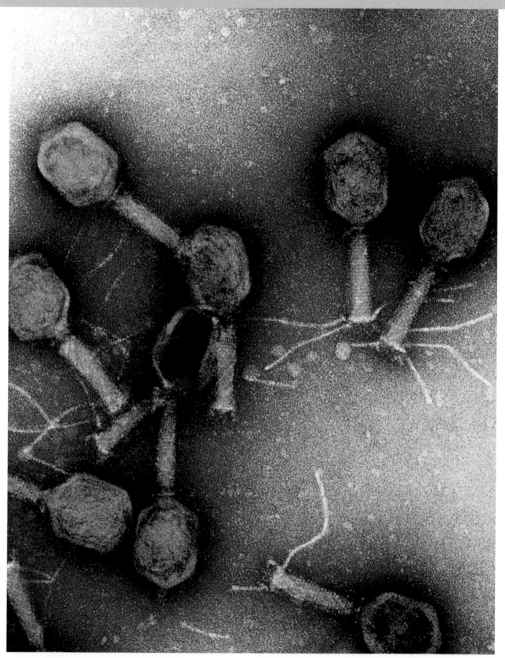

Bacteriophages are viruses that infect bacteria. The virus uses the bacteria's reproductive machinery to make more viruses. In the process, the bacteria is killed and more bacteriophages are produced. Some scientists believe that bacteriophages may be the key to a new class of antibiotics.

tions lies in their specificity. A bacteriophage will only infect a specific strain of bacteria, meaning that doctors would need to know exactly which bacteria is making a patient sick. Determining the strain of bacteria is generally carried out in the hospital's laboratory, and it can take time—sometimes more time than a patient has.

Managing Antibiotics

Scientists are working on developing new antibiotics in order to maintain a pool of them that work. However, to keep these antibiotics effective, doctors may have to limit how they prescribe them. In addition, people may have to change the way they view some illnesses. For example, sometimes a person takes antibiotics too readily, before giving the body a chance to defeat the bacteria on its own. In these cases, bacteria are being exposed to antibiotics needlessly. Given another few days, the body's natural immune system would likely have taken care of the problem.

People also need to be aware of which illnesses require an antibiotic and which do not. Taking an antibiotic when you have the flu, for example, even if you are prescribed one, will not help. In fact, as explained earlier, it can do a lot of harm, because more bacteria in your body would be exposed to that antibiotic.

Another way people can help is by following the doctor's instructions when taking the antibiotic that has been prescribed. Sometimes an antibiotic really is needed. However, if the entire course of the medication is not taken as the doctor prescribes, the antibiotic cannot work optimally. Antibiotics must be present in the bloodstream in a certain amount before they can work. If the entire course of the antibiotic is not taken, this level is never reached. Sometimes people stop taking the drug prescribed to them when they start to feel better. However, a lessening in symptoms does not mean that all of the bacteria have been killed. Plus, the bacteria that are left behind have been exposed to the antibiotic and may develop resistance.

Governments may have to change regulations regarding the way antibiotics are used in animals. Using antibiotics to cure sick animals of infection is not the problem. But giving healthy animals antibiotics on the off chance that an infection might occur, or to promote growth, raises concerns.

The discovery of antibiotics brought about revolutionary changes in medicine. These drugs have saved many lives and continue to save lives today. In the future, if we all work together—scientists, farmers, doctors, and patients—we can curb the emergence of drug-resistant bacteria and keep antibiotics working for us.

Glossary

antibacterials Synthetic chemicals that mimic the action of antibiotics.

antibiotic A naturally occurring product of a microorganism that can kill or slow the growth of bacteria.

antibodies Complex chemicals produced by the B cells of the immune system that recognize and identify a particular antigen for destruction.

antigens Chemicals on the surface of bacteria and other microorganisms that are recognized by the immune system.

antimicrobials General term for medications that kill or slow the growth of microorganisms.

antiviral Describes medications used to treat illnesses, such as the common cold, caused by viruses.

bacteria Tiny, single-celled, living organisms that can sometimes cause illness in plants, animals, and humans.

bactericides Substances or agents, such as antibiotics, that kill bacteria.

bacteriophages Viruses that infect and kill bacteria.

bacteriostatic Describes a substance, such as an antibiotic, that prevents bacteria from multiplying.

community-acquired Refers to an infection that affects a healthy person outside of the hospital.

DNA The chemical molecule that carries genetic information from generation to generation.

hormones Chemical messengers that relay signals from one body cell to another.

immune system A group of organs, tissues, and cells that work together to protect the body from invading microorganisms and other foreign particles.

leukocytes White blood cells that search for and destroy pathogenic microorganisms in the body.

microorganisms Tiny organisms that are too small to be seen without the aid of a microscope.

mutations Changes in the DNA, or genetic material, of an organism.

pathogenic Capable of causing illness.

plasmids Small pieces of DNA that can be transferred from one bacterium to another.

superbugs Bacteria that are resistant to all known antibiotics.

Find Out More

Books

Ballard, Carol. *From Cowpox to Antibiotics: Discovering Vaccines and Medicines.* Chicago: Heinemann-Raintree, 2006.

Goldsmith, Connie. *Superbugs Strike Back: When Antibiotics Fail.* Minneapolis: Twenty-First Century Books, 2007.

Guilfoile, Patrick. *Antibiotic-Resistant Bacteria.* New York: Chelsea House Publications, 2007.

Klosterman, Lorrie. *Drug-Resistant Superbugs.* New York: Marshall Cavendish Benchmark, 2010.

———. *Immune System.* New York: Marshall Cavendish Benchmark, 2009.

Watson, Stephanie. *Superbugs: The Rise of Drug-Resistant Germs.* New York: Rosen Publishing Group, 2010.

Websites

The Immune System

www.cyh.sa.gov.au/HealthTopics/HealthTopicDetailsKids.
aspx?p=335&np=152&id=2402

This Australian site explains how your immune system knows which cells to attack and other topics related to the immune system.

KidsHealth: A Kid's Guide to Shots

http://kidshealth.org/kid/stay_healthy/body/guide_shots.html

This site explains how vaccinations work and why you need them.

KidsHealth: Chilling Out with Colds

http://kidshealth.org/kid/stay_healthy/body/colds.html

KidsHealth has a whole section dedicated to colds, from what a cold is to how to speed up your recovery.

KidsHealth: Your Immune System

http://kidshealth.org/kid/htbw/immune.html

Another helpful guide from KidsHealth provides information on the immune system.

What about Antibiotics?

www.cyh.sa.gov.au/HealthTopics/HealthTopicDetailsKids.
aspx?p=335&np=285&id=2376

This site explains how antibiotics work, when you need them, and when you don't.

Index

Page numbers in **boldface** are illustrations.

About the Author

Kristi Lew is the author of more than thirty science books for teachers and young people. Fascinated with science from a young age, she studied biochemistry and genetics in college. Before she started writing full-time, she worked in genetics laboratories and taught high school science. Kristi has written several books, including *Respiratory System* in The Amazing Human Body series and *Volt* in the Green Cars series. She lives in St. Petersburg, Florida, and enjoys sailing with her husband aboard their small sailboat, *Proton.*